WHAT WOULD

OZZY

DO?

OUTRAGEOUS AFFIRMATIONS AND ADVICE
FROM THE PRINCE OF DARKNESS

POP PRESS

Pop Press, an imprint of Ebury Publishing
20 Vauxhall Bridge Road
London SW1V 2SA

Pop Press is part of the Penguin Random House group of companies
whose addresses can be found at global.penguinrandomhouse.com

Penguin
Random House
UK

Copyright © Pop Press 2024

First published by Pop Press in 2024

Design: Ed Pickford
Text: Liz Marvin
Illustrations: Ollie Mann

www.penguin.co.uk

A CIP catalogue record for this book is available from the British Library

ISBN: 9781529933284

Typeset in 10/14pt ITC Franklin Gothic LT Pro by Jouve (UK), Milton Keynes
Printed and bound in Great Britain by TJ Books Ltd, Padstow, Cornwall

The authorised representative in the EEA is Penguin Random House
Ireland, Morrison Chambers, 32 Nassau Street, Dublin D02 YH68

MIX
Paper | Supporting
responsible forestry
FSC
www.fsc.org   FSC® C018179

Penguin Random House is committed to a
sustainable future for our business, our readers
and our planet. This book is made from Forest
Stewardship Council® certified paper.

'If you have a fucking dream, don't stop believing in it.'

– Ozzy Osbourne

CONTENTS

INTRODUCTION

THE WONDERFUL WISDOM OF OZZY OSBOURNE

With his band Black Sabbath, Ozzy Osbourne was a pioneer of heavy metal, taking the noise and intensity of the Birmingham factories where they worked and turning it into music that earned them fans around the world. But this is only one of the reasons why we love Ozzy. He has been through a lot and been open about his problems. He might be known for his wild-man stage persona, but underneath it all, he's a dedicated family man who has always found a way to get back up when life has knocked him down, with his trademark wit and humour.

Modest as he is, Ozzy might be surprised to hear it, but there is a lot we can learn from the Prince of Darkness . . .

LIVE IN THE MOMENT

A big part of Black Sabbath's success comes from their charismatic frontman's incredible stage presence. Ozzy loves performing and fans never fail to get swept up in his energy and love for what he does. He believes that when you don't know what's around the corner, it's all about getting everything you can out of today.

PUSH THE BOUNDARIES

Unsurprisingly, Ozzy is not big on conformity. When you've had a hand in sparking a whole new musical genre you're unlikely to be someone who plays by the rules. Plenty of people were appalled by Black Sabbath's music and image but Ozzy has never cared about trying to please. So long as he's pursuing his own creative passions, having fun and playing great gigs, that's enough for Ozzy.

STAY TRUE TO YOURSELF

And you can only be your best creatively if you stay true to who you are. Sure, Ozzy may have been caught up in rock 'n' roll excess in his life but he's never forgotten where he came from. Even when eating sausage and mash cooked by a chef in his Hollywood mansion he's remembered his roots, never losing his wry sense of humour or keen awareness of absurdity.

GET BACK UP AGAIN

As well as the addiction issues that he's had to face, Ozzy has been through a lot, from grief to serious accidents and health problems that have left him in excruciating pain. But – with the help of those who love him – Ozzy has always found a way to get back on his feet and keep going.

APPRECIATE FAMILY

Ozzy may be the self-styled Prince of Darkness but he's also a proud husband, dad and granddad. Maybe the weirdest thing about Ozzy Osbourne is that he's actually a pretty normal guy. He never misses an opportunity to credit his wife Sharon, the love of his life, for all she's done for him or tell the world how much he loves his kids. The only thing that matters more to him than music is his family.

MUSIC

'Rock and roll is for the people. And I love people. That's what I'm about.'

'Music is a good release
from a lot of things
in life.'

'A great gig is better
than any sex or drug.'

'I never said I was a great singer, I just had fun.'

'I'm just absolutely thrilled just to be on stage and playing for people that wanna see me.'

'The only animal you'll see on stage now is Ozzy Osbourne.'

'I was blessed to work with some of the greatest musicians in the world.'

'Doing a live show is
what I live for.'

[On his career] 'I started in 1968 and I've worked at it since then. It's just been fantastic.'

CREATIVITY

'I've always got to be doing *something*. I can't sit still, me.'

'We all want to communicate with our fellow man, but we're too frightened to try.'

'If I get a melody in my head, I have to record it straight away.'

'The best record is
always the one you
do next.'

'I thought I'd never write again without any stimulation. But you know what? Instead of picking up the bottle I just got honest and said, "I don't want life to go [to pieces]".'

'Rock music is not meant to be perfect. Nowadays everyone irons the fucking air, it's all about technology.'

'Do what you can, even
if it's a little, just so
you're doing stuff.'

'When you've got all the
yachts and all those
things or whatever,
you've still got to
have a passion.'

'If you wanna do
anything in this world
you gotta really wanna.'

'Don't give a fuck and
just do what you like.'

FAMILY

'I love you all. I love you more than life itself. You're all fucking mad.'

'Without my Sharon,
I'd be fucking gone.'

'My father was a fucking gem. I got my front from my father and my singing voice from my mother.'

'All I ever wanted to do was to do something good so that my parents could be proud of me.'

'Behind me, my wife pulls my strings.'

'I've come to the conclusion that people don't want to know the truth – that I'm a happily married man with kids who I absolutely adore, and that what I do is entertain people. I am not fucking Dracula.'

'When I was a kid, if my father told me not to do anything I would immediately run out and do it.'

FRIENDS AND IDOLS

'Life's too short to
have enemies.'

'You learn who your
friends are when the
shit hits the fan.'

'My rock god is Lemmy Kilmister. He shot from the hip every time.'

'[Randy Rhoads] was not only a great rock and roll player, but in the classics, and in every other field, he was phenomenal . . . I loved him in an instant.'

'Tony Iommi is the finest guitar player . . . he can't stop coming up with these incredible riffs.'

'Elton [John] is a sweetheart. You would be surprised, when you are feeling miserable you find out who is a friend and who doesn't give a shit.'

'Andrew [Watt] and I always start off friendly. We fall out. We get back together again. At the end of the day you get married to it.'

'Steve Jones of the Sex Pistols once said to me, "I hated The Beatles." To me, that's like saying you hate air.'

'Meeting Paul McCartney was fucking phenomenal. I tried to get him to play bass on one of my songs. But he said he couldn't improve on the bassline that was there. I said, "Are you kidding? You could piss on the record and I'd make it my life."'

'I remember listening to the first Zeppelin album. It was like such a great breath of fresh air for somebody doing something acceptable but yet so different.'

LOVE

'I wasn't exactly Romeo
at school. Most chicks
thought I was insane.'

'If my wife said we've
got to go and live in
Timbuktu, I'll go.'

'The love I have for what I've been able to do with people is unbelievable! I've affected people's lives, you know!'

'What Sharon would do
to try to stop me
drinking was take my
clothes. So if I wanted to
get a drink I'd have to
dress up in hers.'

'I think it's important to say to your kids that you love them. I try to tell my kids that I love them every day.'

'The relationship I have
with my audience is the
biggest love affair of
my life.'

PHILOSOPHY

'I don't know what's going to happen tomorrow and I can't re-live yesterday but I live in the moment.'

'I'm trying to get as
much done as I can
before the ultimate
final curtain.'

'I think entertainers should stay entertainers and politicians should stay liars.'

'I can only do what
I believe in. If I was a
fake at what I was doing,
I couldn't do it.'

'You've got to be careful what you say in this world, because it'll come back to kick you in the pants.'

'Whatever happens,
I won't let the world
forget about me!'

'I don't like to treat
people any less than
I would like to be
treated myself.'

'Everyone thinks I'm
fucking hilarious but
the thing is that I'm not
trying to be funny.
I'm just being me!'

'I'd rather have people get rid of their aggression at an Ozzy concert than by beating some old lady over the head and running off with her purse.'

'Being on the recovery programme, you have to have a power greater than yourself. You can call it God, or nature, the ocean, anything.'

'If you can laugh at your mistakes, it's a good thing.'

'The power of people,
when they focus on
something positive,
never fails to amaze me.'

FAME

'Lock up your dogs,
cats and daughters,
Ozzy's coming!'

[On continuing to perform while recovering from surgery] 'Sharon said to me: "They've asked you to close the Commonwealth Games," and I said: "Sharon, I can't even fucking stand up!"'

'I'm just a normal guy
like everybody else.'

'I don't go out and turn
people into Satanists
or anything.'

'In this world, for some reason, you have to do some pretty bizarre things before people begin to know what you're about.'

'If people recognise me
I'll get very humble but,
at the same time, if they
don't recognise me I get
kinda upset.'

'One of the few good things about being dyslexic is that when I say I don't read reviews, I mean I don't read reviews.'

'I've been accused of everything. I was going to have a t-shirt made up that would have said, "If your day's totally screwed up, blame Ozzy Osbourne".'

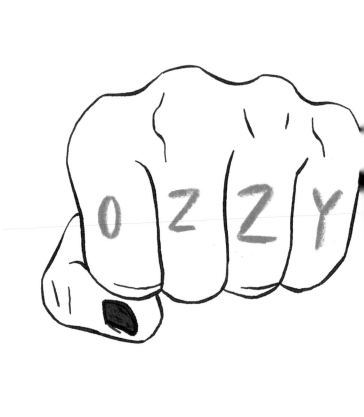

SUCCESS

'I'd like to be remembered for the work I did with Black Sabbath. I'm so proud of the music. But to be honest, just being remembered would be an achievement to me.'

'Coming from a working-class background, I hate to let people down. I hate to not do my job.'

'I felt like a right twat having a chef. What's a fucking hors d'oeuvre? A bacon sandwich and a fucking cup of tea, that'll do me.'

'I'm here for people, to
give enjoyment, to give
them my life, my soul,
my everything.'

'I've had so many brushes with death that I'm the Comeback Kid. If I was a cat I'd have 33 lives.'

'You don't just give up at the first sign of choppy waters; you carry on rowing.'

'You know the time when I will retire? When I can hear them nail a lid on my box. And then I'll fucking do an encore. I'm the Prince of Darkness.'

'I never thought I'd get further than Aston.'

SURVIVAL

'It takes a lot to hold
me down.'

Ozzy: We took LSD, we took cocaine. We took vast amounts of marijuana. It was fun at the time but then we thought, 'This isn't a very good idea any more.'

Interviewer: So you have a more stable life now?

Ozzy: No!

'I was doing a driver's test once and I woke up and the door was open, the car was parked and there was a note: "Mr Osbourne, you've failed and I suggest you don't try to drive this vehicle any further".'

'I'm not ashamed of anything that I've done in the past. We all have a little bit of a skeleton in our cupboard that we think, fuck, I don't want to talk about that again. But it don't really bother me.'

'When you're in the eye
of the storm you don't
realise you're screwed;
all I was trying to do
was survive.'

'Years ago, a doctor told me I was going to be dead before the end of the year. Keith Richards has a few more lives on me, though. I don't understand why his body hasn't just fucking stopped yet.'

'The taste of bats is
very salty.'

'I took ten tabs of acid then went for a walk in a field. I stood there talking to this horse for about an hour. In the end, the horse turned round and told me to fuck off.'

'My bad ideas got me
into rehab. Many times.'

'Sharon said, "I've found this place called the Betty Ford Center where they teach you to drink like a gentleman." I'm thinking, "Well, that's it, that's always been my problem. I've been doing it wrong."'

'When you're on the bottle, you don't realise you're as bad as you are.'

FRIENDS AND FANS

'It's fascinating that the
singer of the band that's
known for being so dark
and so evil could be
so loveable.'

– Dave Grohl

'Most fans thought he lived in a big, dark castle with skeletons in the cellar.'

– Alice Cooper

'Sitting next to Ozzy while he's writing lyrics and practising the vocal is really fuckin' a trip. I've been listening to Ozzy since I was like 13 years old.'

– Slash

'I think Ozzy's music is timeless. It makes me cry and gives me the chills.'

– Post Malone

'Ozzy was a genius for coming up with the melodies that he did . . . he usually wrote right off the top of his head.'

– Geezer Butler

'Ozzy was my introduction to heavy metal music. He's a true inspiration and a hero of mine.'

– Jack Black

'He is the most
irresistible madman
you will ever meet in
your life.'

– Kelly Osbourne

ACKNOWLEDGEMENTS

P10 from Late Show with David Letterman, March 25, 1982. P11 from Classic Rock, 'Ozzy Osbourne: I don't plan on going anywhere, but my time's going to come' (2022). P12 from Yahoo Entertainment, 'Ozzy Osbourne talks health issues, comeback albums and hopes for 2023' (2023. P13 from NME, 'The Big Read – Ozzy Osbourne: "This album saved my life"' (2020). P14 from The Tapes Archive, 'Ozzy Osbourne' (1997). P15 from Late Show with David Letterman, March 25, 1982. P16 from NME, 'Ozzy Osbourne on his double Grammy win: "I'm one lucky motherfucker"' (2023). P17 from Metal Hammer, 'Ozzy Osbourne will play more shows even if he has to be wheeled out on stage: "it's not a job, it's a ***ing passion!"' (2023). P18 from Spin, 'Ozzy Osbourne On Health, Podcasts, Reality TV And A Half-Century Of Rock' (2023). P22 from Kerrang, 'Ozzy Osbourne: "If I drop dead now, at least I can't say that I've had a dull career"' (2022). P23 from Guitar World, 'The Good, The Bad & The Ozzy: Or How to Become a Heavy Metal Guitar Hero in One E-Z Lesson.' (1990). P24 from GQ, 'Ozzy Osbourne: I'm a happily married man with three kids. I'm not Dracula" (2004). P25 from Classic Rock, ' "I've done my best, and I'm happy" - How Ozzy Osbourne made Patient Number 9' (2022). P26 from Billboard, 'Back in 'Black" (2007). P27 from The Guardian, 'Ozzy Osbourne: 'I had nothing to lose" (2011). P28 from Rolling Stone, 'Ozzy Osbourne on His Road Back From Hell: 'I Was Absolutely in Agony" (2019). P29 from Elsewhere.co.nz, 'Ozzy Osbourne Interviewed' (1997). P30 from The Howard Stern Show, (1996). P31 from NME, 'The Big Read – Ozzy Osbourne: "This album saved my life"' (2020).

WHAT WOULD OZZY DO?

P34 from The Osbournes, 'Series 1 Episode 1: There Goes The Neighbourhood' (2002). P35 from The Guardian, 'Tea with Ozzy Osbourne: 'I've sung that song for 55 years. I'm not going to forget the words" (2022). P36 from Medium, 'Interview with Ozzy Osbourne' (1982). P37 from GQ, 'Ozzy Osbourne: I'm a happily married man with three kids. I'm not Dracula" (2004). P38 from Billboard News, 'Ozzy Osbourne On Grammy Nominations, Working With Jeff Beck, Eric Clapton & More' (2023). P39 from GQ, 'Ozzy Osbourne: I'm a happily married man with three kids. I'm not Dracula" (2004). P40 from Guitar World, 'Badfellas' (1997). P44 from Classic Rock, 'Ozzy Osbourne: I don't plan on going anywhere, but my time's going to come' (2022). P45 from Ozzy Osbourne, 'I am Ozzy' (2010). P46 from BBC, 'The Rock Show with Johnnie Walker – Monday 18 June 2018'. P47 from Guitar Player,' Ozzy Osbourne Shares His Fond Memories of Randy Rhoads in 1982 GP Interview' (1982). P48 from Planet Rock, 'Ozzy Osbourne hails Tony Iommi as 'the finest guitar player" (2022). P49 from The Sun, "BOURNE AGAIN Ozzy Osbourne, 70, admits he's lucky to be alive after wild rock 'n' roll lifestyle featuring drug overdoses and quad bike crash' (2019). P50 from Kerrang, 'Ozzy Osbourne: "If I drop dead now, at least I can't say that I've had a dull career" ' (2022). P51 from Rolling Stone India, 'From The Archives: Ozzy Osbourne' (2015). P52 from Farout Magazine, 'The reason why Paul McCartney turned down Ozzy Osbourne collaboration' (2022). P53 from The History of Rock'n'Roll – created by Andrew Solt, Quincy Jones (1995). P56 from Ozzy Osbourne, 'I am Ozzy' (2010).P57 from Vanity Fair, ' "It's F–cking Crazy": Ozzy Osbourne Is Done With America' (2022). P58 from Paste Magazine, ' "I've Always Got Demons": Ozzy Osbourne on Patient Number 9' (2022). P59 from Independent on Sunday, 'The Ozzmosis of Ozzy Osbourne' (1995). P60 from GQ, 'Ozzy Osbourne: If I'd have gone to church I'd still be there now, confessing all my sins!" (2020). P61 from People, 'Ozzy Osbourne Is Determined to Tour Again After 'Nightmare'

ACKNOWLEDGEMENTS

Health Setbacks: 'Survival Is My Legacy" (2022). P64 from Esquire, 'Ozzy Osbourne: I'm the Luckiest Man in the World' (2014). P65 from The Independent, 'The Saturday Interview – Ozzy Osbourne' (2022). P66 from NME, 'Ozzy Osbourne criticises politicians in the wake of Nelson Mandela's death' (2013). P67 from Spin, 'Ozzy Osbourne on being Ozzy' (1986). P68 from Blabbermouth.net, 'Ozzy Osboune Talks 'Scream', Possibility Of Retirement' (2010). P69 from Classic Rock, ' "I've done my best, and I'm happy" - How Ozzy Osbourne made Patient Number 9' (2022). P70 from Classic Rock, 'Ozzy Osbourne: I wish I was a hero to myself' (2022). P71 from Hot Press, 'Happy Birthday Ozzy Osbourne' (2002). P72 from Spin, 'Ozzy Osbourne on being Ozzy' (1986).P73 from Good Morning Britain, 3 March 2020. P74 from NOLA.com, 'The Ozzy Osbourne interview: his new 'Memoirs,' Black Sabbath, Halloween and Paul McCartney' (2014). P75 from Ozzy Osbourne, 'I am Ozzy' (2010). P78 from Metal Edge, 'Ozzy Osbourne: Outrageous as Ever!' (1986). P79 from from The Independent, 'The Saturday Interview – Ozzy Osbourne' (2022). P80. From Classic Rock, 'Ozzy Osbourne denies he's the Antichrist while dressed as Dracula in a coffin' (2022). P81 from Ear of Newt, 'That time Ozzy Osbourne told me that he wasn't "a f***ing warlock" trying to turn people into satanists' (1984). P82 from Mojo, 'MOJO Time Machine: Ozzy Osbourne Bites The Head Off A Dove!' (1981). P83 from BBC News, 'Ozzy Osbourne's final Interview as Black Sabbath frontman'(2017). P84 from Ozzy Osbourne, 'I am Ozzy' (2010). P85 from Whoopi Goldberg Show (1993). P88 from The Guardian, 'Ozzy Osbourne: 'My problem, really, is I don't remember I'm 70" (2018). P89 from Good Morning America, 'Ozzy Osbourne breaks his silence on his battle with Parkinson's disease' (2020). P90 from Fame & Fortune (1997). P91 from Night Flight (1992). P92 from from The Sun, "BOURNE AGAIN Ozzy Osbourne, 70, admits he's lucky to be alive after wild rock 'n' roll lifestyle featuring drug overdoses and quad bike crash' (2019).P93 from NME, 'Ozzy

Osbourne: 'Knighthood would be great' (2014). P94 from The Mail Online, 'Ozzy Osbourne embraces his grey locks as he chats to pals while leaning on his cane for support' (2020). P95 from NME, 'Ozzy Osbourne: 'Knighthood would be great'(2014). P98 from Billboard, 'Icon Ozzy Osbourne On His Grammy Nominations, Working With Jeff Beck, Eric Clapton & More | Billboard News' (2023). P99 from The Decline of Western Civilisation Part II, directed by Penelope Spheeris (1988). P100 from Planet Radio, 'Ozzy Osbourne reveals he fell asleep on his driving test' (2017). P101 from Spin, 'Ozzy Osbourne: Our 1986 Cover Story' (1986). P102 from British GQ, 'GQ Men of the Year Award 2020' (2020). P103 from Rolling Stone India, 'Ozzy Osbourne' (2010). P104 from Late Show with David Letterman, March 25, 1982. P105 from Classic Rock, 'Ozzy Osbourne gave up LSD after talking to a horse for an hour' (2022). P106 from Daily Mail, 'Ozzy Osbourne reveals Eddie Van Halen once called and asked him to join Van Halen... while reminiscing about the late guitarist's wizardry' (2020). P107 from Rolling Stone India, 'Ozzy Osbourne' (2010). P108 from Rolling Stone India, 'Ozzy Osbourne Opens Up About the Bad Old Days' (2011). P112 from Mojo, 'Man in Black' (2017). P113 from Irish Examiner, 'Cooper brands Ozzy 'a joke'' (2007). P114 from Rolling Stone, 'Slash on Recording With Ozzy and Lemmy, Plans for Summer Tour' (2010). P115 from Alternative Press, 'Post Malone, Rob Zombie talk Ozzy Osbourne's legacy in new doc trailer' (2020). P116 from The Rock Experience with Mike Brunn – Ep 247 (2023). P117 from Metal Hammer, 'We got Tenacious D to interview Ozzy and it turns out even Jack Black gets star struck' (2023). P118 from from Alternative Press, 'Post Malone, Rob Zombie talk Ozzy Osbourne's legacy in new doc trailer' (2020).